PLANETARY EXPLORATION

OUR SUN
AND THE
INNER PLANETS

Don Davis and
Anny Chantal Levasseur-Regourd

Series editor: Dr David Hughes

Facts On File
New York • Oxford

Facts On File, Inc.
460 Park Avenue South
New York NY 10016
USA

Library of Congress Cataloging-in-Publication Data

Levasseur-Regourd, Anny Chantal, Professor
    Our Sun and the inner planets / text, Anny Chantal Levasseur-Regourd;
illustrations, Donald Davis.
        p.   cm. -- (Planetary exploration)
    Includes index.
    Summary: Text and illustrations present what astronomers now know
about the "nuclear powerhouse" that dominates our solar system.
    ISBN 0-8160-2045-0
    1. Sun--Juvenile literature. 2. Solar system--Juvenile
literature. [1. Sun.] I. Davis, Donald, ill. II. Title.
III. Series.
QB521.5.L48   1989
523.7--dc20   89-31689
                                                                 CIP
                                                                        AC

Facts On File books are available at special discounts when
purchased in bulk quantities for businesses, associations,
institutions or sales promotion. Please contact the Special
Sales Department of our New York office at 212/683-2244
(dial 800/322-8755 except in NY, AK or HI).

Designed and produced by BLA Publishing Limited,
East Grinstead, Sussex, England.

A member of the **Ling Kee Group**
LONDON · HONG KONG · TAIPEI · SINGAPORE · NEW YORK

Phototypeset in Britain by BLA Publishing/Composing Operations
Color origination in Hong Kong
Printed and bound in Portugal

10 9 8 7 6 5 4 3 2 1

Note to the reader
In this book some words are printed in **bold** type.
These words are listed in the glossary on page 42.
The glossary gives a brief explanation of words which
may be new to you.

Contents

Foreword

Long before man had the ability to explore space, he imagined what it might be like. Now that our journey beyond the Earth's atmosphere has begun, an artist can draw upon scientific knowledge gathered by probes and satellites in space, and observations made here on Earth, to portray a world where man has never been. Using what scientists know about the violent beginning of our solar system, the artist can take us back into the past to witness the formation of the planets, or into the future to imagine how they might one day be colonized. Through these paintings we can dive into the clouds of Jupiter, hover above the furnace of a sunspot, or even look back on our own solar system as we travel farther away into the galaxy.

In the six volumes of the **Planetary Exploration** series, we have combined the most advanced knowledge about the planets of our solar system with the extraordinary work of a noted space artist. Each book, written by an expert in the field, takes the reader beyond current facts and theories to the frontier of the unknown: the surface of Mars, the rings of Saturn, the tiny glacial world of Pluto, the many moons of Uranus, and beyond. Artist Don Davis has matched these exciting scientific discoveries with vivid illustrations that allow us to "travel" to these planets and unlock their mysteries.

We hope that, in **Planetary Exploration**, you will enjoy sharing this adventure.

David W Hughes

Our domain in space

For more than 4,000 years, astronomers have been observing the sky, trying to understand the mysteries of our solar system. At first, they thought the Earth was at the center of the universe. Then, in 1543 the Polish astronomer Nicolaus Copernicus argued that the Earth, together with the planets known at that time, Mercury, Venus, Jupiter and Saturn, moves around the Sun. In 1609, an astronomer in Italy, Galileo Galilei, discovered that planets reflect sunlight and may have satellites moving around them, just as the Moon circles the Earth. During the same year in Germany, Johann Kepler computed that the paths or orbits of planets are **elliptical**. He found a simple relationship between a planet's average distance from the Sun and its **period of revolution**, the time it takes to complete its orbit.

In the 1950s, the Space Age began. Artificial satellites are now orbiting the Earth and many space probes are traveling

▼ Our Sun lies at the center of a solar system of nine planets, all traveling around it in the same direction. With the exception of the outrider, Pluto, and the innermost planet, Mercury, their paths all lie almost in the same flat **disc**. Planets shine in the sky by scattering sunlight, like a mirror. Ancient astronomers could only see as far as Saturn, the sixth planet from the Sun. Uranus was discovered in 1781, Neptune in 1846 and Pluto in 1930. Most astronomers think that no other large planets will be found beyond Pluto.

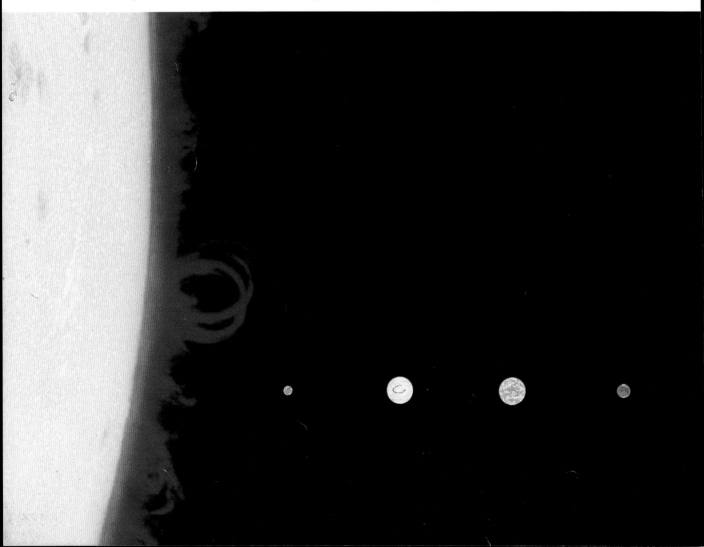

Facts about the solar system

Planet	Diameter in miles (km)	Distance from Sun*	Orbital period (years)
Mercury	3,030 (4,880)	36 (58)	0.3
Venus	7,520 (12,100)	68 (108)	0.6
Earth	7,926 (12,756)	94 (150)	1.0
Mars	4,218 (6,788)	142 (228)	1.9
Jupiter	88,732 (142,796)	483 (778)	11.9
Saturn	74,567 (120,000)	886 (1,426)	29.5
Uranus	32,000 (51,500)	1,790 (2,880)	84.0
Neptune	30,780 (49,500)	2,790 (4,490)	165.0
Pluto	1,420 (2,284)	3,675 (5,900)	249.0

Note: *in million miles (million km)

throughout the solar system. We have discovered a great deal about our Sun, the star which brings light and warmth to our planet, and about the other inhospitable worlds surrounding it. But there is still so much left to learn.

A globe of glowing gases

Our beautiful neighboring star, the Sun, is an enormous sphere of glowing gases, pulled together by **gravity**. As explained in 1666 by Isaac Newton, the British scientist, gravity attracts objects towards each other. It also holds the planets in their paths around the Sun, and the satellites in their paths around the planets.

Astronomers on Earth have been able to discover which gases are found in the Sun by **spectroscopy**. You may have noticed that white light can be split up into the rainbow colors of the visible **spectrum** using a **prism**. Light from glowing gases also behaves in the same way when it passes through a **spectroscope**. The different gases present are characterized by different lines in the spectrum. The Sun is mainly made up of hydrogen, the lightest and simplest of all gases in the universe, and helium the second-lightest gas.

A huge nuclear reactor

Our solar system was born 4,600 million years ago from a swirling cloud of gases and dust in orbit around the center of our Milky Way galaxy. The Sun is around 870,000 miles (1.4 million km) in diameter, over 100 times larger and about 300,000 times heavier than the Earth and works like a huge nuclear furnace. It is so huge that its gravity pulls hydrogen atoms together and deep in the solar **core**, their centers (or nuclei) join in **nuclear fusion**. The hydrogen atoms are changed into helium atoms releasing a tremendous amount of energy. The temperature of the core is an incredible 59 million °F (15 million °C)!

Nuclear energy seeps out slowly from the solar core and gives out light at the golden surface, or **photosphere**. The solar surface is not solid like the Earth's, but its high temperature, about 10,300°F (5,700°C), and **density** make it impossible to see through. The Sun will continue to generate light and heat for 5,000 million years, when most of the hydrogen will have vanished. The Sun will then get cooler and turn into a **red giant** star.

Facts about the Sun	
Diameter	870,000 miles (1,400,000 km)
Mass	300,000 times the Earth's
Volume	1.3 million times the Earth's
Surface gravity	28 times the Earth's
Distance from Earth	94 million miles (150 million km)
Rotation rate	25 days at the equator
Present age	4,600 million years
Life expectancy	10,000 million years
Distance from center of galaxy	30,000 light years
Time to orbit the galaxy	about 250 million years
Distance from nearest star	4.3 light years

◀ The surface of the Sun has a mottled appearance caused by the slightly different temperatures of the swirling and bubbling gas.

The **chromosphere**, a layer of pinkish-colored gases several miles (km) deep surrounds the golden photosphere.

▼ The Milky Way galaxy can be seen from a point near the Sun. The nuclear bulge in the middle of the picture has a reddish-yellow tint because it is mainly made up of older stars. (Stars change color from blue–white to red as they get older.) In the foreground are young, hot, blue stars, dark interstellar dust and pink clouds of hydrogen.

The Sun's ruby crown

The Sun's glowing surface prevents us from seeing the thin outer layers of gases which surround it. The elusive solar outer atmosphere can only be seen if the photosphere is hidden, which happens during a solar **eclipse** when the Moon passes between the Earth and the Sun.

The darkened solar disc is surrounded by a **corona**, a cloud or halo of gases which splendidly crowns the Sun. Immediately before or after the eclipse, the chromosphere, a ruby-colored, fiery ring of gases, can be seen around the edges of the disc. **Prominences**, giant hydrogen jets, may surge up into the corona or loop downwards through the chromosphere, making the eclipse still more spectacular.

▶ As the Moon orbits the Earth it sometimes passes directly between the Earth and the Sun. The shadow cast by the Moon just touches the Earth's surface. People in that small shadow region can see the Sun in eclipse.

◀ The corona of the Sun is a tenuous outer atmosphere of highly-**ionized**, superhot gas. It is only one-millionth as bright as the surface of the Sun, and it is best seen at the time of a solar eclipse. The shape of the corona is determined by the solar magnetic field. The black image in the center is the back of the Moon as it passes between the Earth and the Sun. Gas in the corona streams away from the Sun, past the planets on its way to the edge of the solar system and beyond.

"Baily's Beads," a string of bright spots around the edge of the Moon are caused by sunlight peeping through the valleys and craters on the Moon's surface.

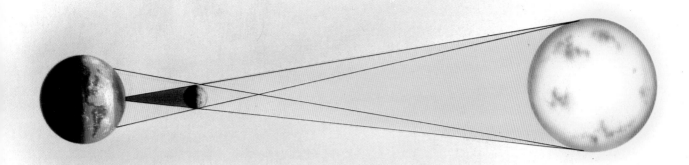

▼ The Moon casts an elliptical shadow, which races across the Earth's surface as the Moon moves along its orbit. The shadow travels along a different path in each eclipse. The one pictured here is a total eclipse that took place on February 26, 1979, when the shadow took only 100 minutes to move from Greenland to California (along the black path). At any point, the total eclipse lasts only for a few minutes. Observers in the regions above and below the black band can see the Sun only partially covered by the Moon. People outside the hatched region would see no eclipse at all.

An extraordinary event

The solar eclipse is an extraordinary event and does not happen each time the Moon goes around the Earth. The Moon's orbit is tilted with respect to the **orbital plane** of the Earth, so it usually passes above or below, instead of in front of, the Sun. The Earth's orbital plane is called the ecliptic plane, because eclipses only occur when the Moon is close to it.

About twice a year the Moon passes in front of the Sun for a few minutes. When the Moon completely blocks out the Sun's light, at its center, the result is a total eclipse, only visible from a small part of our planet. Beyond this region only part of the Sun is blocked out. The Moon's shadow is then not so dark and the eclipse is termed partial, and can be seen over a much wider area of the Earth.

The next total solar eclipse will be visible on July 22, 1990, between northern Siberia and Finland, followed by one on July 11, 1991 between Mexico and Hawaii, and June 30, 1992, over the southern Atlantic Ocean.

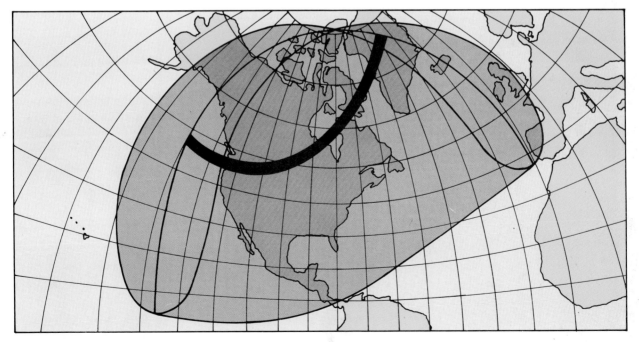

A lunar eclipse

It is surprising that our small satellite, the Moon, can hide the huge Sun, which is 400 times bigger. Because the Moon is much closer to us, the ratio of diameter to distance is about the same, so the Moon looks the same size as the Sun. This is its **angular diameter**, and is about half a degree.

If you were an astronaut working on the Moon, the Earth would seem almost four times wider than the Sun, and its angular diameter would be about 2°. At night, you would marvel at the earthlight shining beautifully on the landscape.

About twice a year, the Earth passes between the Moon and the Sun, and a solar eclipse is visible from the Moon, with the Earth hiding both the solar disc and the inner corona. At the same time on Earth, a lunar eclipse would be seen: the bright, full Moon traveling into the Earth's shadow, turning dark and reddish for a few hours.

▼ These three paintings show the sky viewed from the edge of the same lunar crater. In the picture below it is lunar day, but the whole Moon is in the shadow of the Earth. From Earth we see this as a lunar eclipse. The globe in the sky is planet Earth.

The picture, top right, shows the more usual scene of daytime on the Moon. The Sun is high in the sky and is not eclipsed. To its left can be seen the crescent Earth.

The picture at bottom right shows the lunar night. The only source of light is the full Earth.

Observing an eclipse

The region on Earth within which a total solar eclipse is visible at a given time is less than 190 miles (300 km) wide. The partial eclipse can be seen from a band which is about 3,100 miles (5,000 km) wide.

The spot on Earth from where a total eclipse is visible moves swiftly across the surface as the Earth rotates. At any specific location an increasing partial eclipse comes first, lasting about one hour, followed by the total eclipse, which is only a few minutes long. Finally a decreasing partial eclipse is visible again for about one hour.

Astronomers travel far away to observe a solar eclipse. They may also use special telescopes, **coronagraphs**, which mask out the Sun's disc. These are more effective on mountains or in space, because they work better when the Earth's atmosphere is very thin. Coronagraphs on board satellites can study both the visible and invisible light which comes from the Sun. Some invisible light (**ultraviolet**, X-rays), which would be harmful to life on Earth, is blocked by our atmosphere, but its study tells us a lot about the Sun.

Never look directly at the Sun, even during a partial eclipse; it is so bright that it would damage your eyes and could blind you.

▶ The following sequence of views shows an eclipse in India. In this eclipse, the Moon appears to move across the Sun from bottom to top. The illumination of the ground decreases only slightly during the time taken for the Moon to cover the first half of the Sun. When more than four-fifths of the solar disc is masked by the Moon, the Earth's surface is rapidly shrouded in darkness. After a few minutes the orb of the Sun appears again, and light and normality return.

Dark spots on the Sun

If it were not too dangerous to view the Sun through a large telescope, you would be able to see some grains, or granules, expanding and fading in just a few minutes. These originate in the photosphere, which moves by **convection** like the surface of boiling water. Forming the image of the Sun on a screen from a telescope, you might see elongated dark patches or **sunspots**, stretching 60,000 miles (100,000 km) over the photospheric surface. From Earth the dark spots appear to shift a little from day to day showing that the Sun is slowly spinning. It has an equator and a **polar axis**, just like the Earth. The time taken to complete one revolution is its **period of rotation**. Because the Sun is not a solid globe but a ball of gas, its period of rotation varies from about 25 days at the equator to about 30 days near the poles.

An active and changing Sun

Day after day, year after year, solar astronomers have been watching the dark sunspots and noting how their number increases and decreases in an 11-year cycle. A maximum number was found in 1979, and it is anticipated that another

▼ Hovering above the surface of the Sun, we are looking at a cauldron of bubbling gas. The magnetic activity of the solar surface varies through an 11-year cycle. Here it is particularly active and there are many sunspots on the surface. These darker spots are regions with an intense magnetic field and are cooler than the rest of the surface The central region of the spot is known as the **umbra** (Latin for shadow), surrounded by the **penumbra**, which contains "spokes" of hotter material. Note that the spots would be round if we were looking vertically down on them. The granulation on the solar surface is caused by the rising bubbles of hot gas.

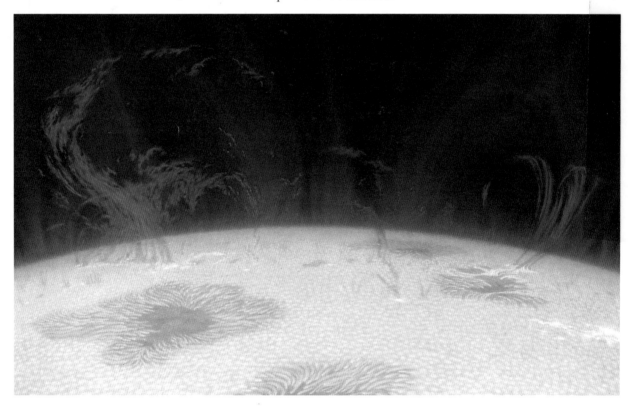

▶ The Sun is a ball of gas getting hotter and denser towards its core. At the center the density is about 160 times greater than that of water, and the temperature is 59 million°F (15 million°C). Nuclear fusion takes place in the core, producing all of the Sun's energy. Surrounding the core is a region through which the heat is transported by radiation, a slow process taking many millions of years, which explains why the Sun is such a steady star. In the outer 10 percent of the Sun the heat is moved by convection and bubbles of hot gas rise to the surface, cool and then fall back. Due to the large gravitational fields, the Sun has a very distinct edge. Wispy **streamers** can be seen moving through the corona.

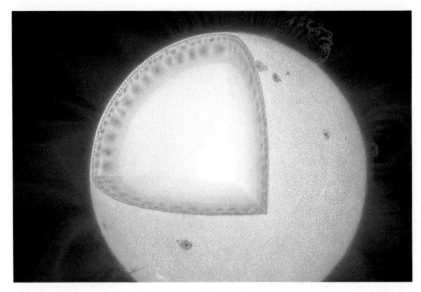

maximum will occur around 1990. Their average number may vary from cycle to cycle.

Sunspots are mysterious, cooler regions of the photosphere, about 7,200°F (4,000°C) rather than the 10,300°F (5,700°C) of the rest of the surface. They are triggered by strong magnetic forces, which pull at solar gases as a magnet pulls at iron. They could account for changes in our weather and climate. Ice ages may have occurred on Earth when solar activity was low.

A wind blowing from the Sun

Conditions on our planet are affected by the changing Sun, both because the visible and ultraviolet light reaching us changes and because the amount of tiny atomic particles that the Sun blows out over the solar system changes. The temperature of the corona is about 3.6 million °F (2 million °C) and this superhot gas is able to escape the Sun's gravity. A solar wind of electrically-charged hydrogen and helium atoms blows outward into space.

Sometimes, an incredibly violent explosion, or **flare**, occurs above a sunspot. An immense amount of energy is released and prominences leap into the solar corona. Streams of energetic particles are injected into the solar wind at 600 miles a second (1,000 km a second), 5,000 times faster than the speed of a jet plane. When the blast of the flare reaches Earth, one and a half days later, the needle of a compass may flicker, and northern lights, or **auroras**, may glow in the night sky.

The Sun's energy greatly affects our environment and our lives, but we do not completely understand it. What is happening in its core? How is the photosphere moving? Why is the corona so hot? Satellites and space probes of the future will play a great role in unraveling the Sun's mysteries.

Mercury

Closest to the Sun, Mercury is a barren world. Its orbit is elliptical, its nearest point to the Sun being 29 million miles (46 million km), stretching to a maximum distance of 43 million miles (70 million km). The mercurian year, the time it takes to complete one orbit, is only 88 Earth days long.

Mercury is hard to see from Earth. It orbits close to the Sun and the angle between the Sun and Mercury as seen from Earth is always smaller than 25°. During the day, the planet is almost impossible to observe in sunlight, while at night, after sunset or before sunrise, it is low on our horizon.

Once Mercury's orbit and angular diameter are known, its size can be computed. With a diameter of 3,030 miles (4,880 km), less than half the Earth's, Mercury is the second smallest of the nine planets (after Pluto) known to be orbiting the Sun.

Mercury's period of rotation around its axis was determined only in the early 1960s, not by difficult visual observation but by **radar**. A radio wave aimed at Mercury is reflected back to Earth by the planet's solid surface. Light, radio and sound waves each have a given **frequency**. (You may have noticed when a fire engine, ambulance or police car speeds past you, its siren seems to change to a lower pitch or frequency. The variation in frequency is related to the speed of the car.) By bouncing radio waves from Earth onto the edge of Mercury, scientists measure the variations in frequency of the reflected waves, which tells them both the speed of the planet and its period of rotation.

It takes Mercury 59 Earth days to rotate once around its axis. During that time it has traveled two-thirds of its orbit about the Sun. So, the length of time between noon on one day and noon on the following day is 176 Earth days. Mercury is the only known planet on which the day is longer than the year.

Facts about Mercury	
Diameter	3,030 miles (4,880 km)
Mass	1/16 of the Earth's
Distance from the Sun	36 million miles (58 million km) (average)
Period of rotation	58.65 days
Orbital period	87.97 days
Inclination of equator	0°
Surface gravity	2/5 of the Earth's
Temperature	750°F (400°C) day −330°F (−200°C) (night)
Atmosphere	negligible

Earth   Mercury

► The surface of Mercury bakes under the glaring Sun and resembles the heavily-cratered far side of the Moon. The Caloris Basin is the largest impact feature that has been discovered so far on Mercury. In this picture it can be seen disappearing into the night side of the planet.

◄ The Earth and Mercury are shown to scale. Mercury's mass is 16 times smaller than Earth's.

A single exploration

Most of our information about Mercury's surface came from the Mariner 10 probe, an unmanned US spacecraft carrying automatic cameras and instruments that radioed its observations back to Earth.

Mariner 10 was launched in November 1973, reaching Mercury's neighboring planet, Venus, in February 1974. It used the venusian gravity to swing into a smaller orbit around the Sun which enabled it to fly past Mercury three times. In March 1975, it was only 205 miles (330 km) above the rocky surface of Mercury.

▼ The American planetary probe, Mariner 10 is depicted in this artist's impression as it would have appeared flying by Mercury on March 29, 1974. It is only 430 miles (690 km) above the surface, its main task is to take a series of pictures and to measure the temperature. Other instruments measure the magnetic fields and ionized gases around the planet.

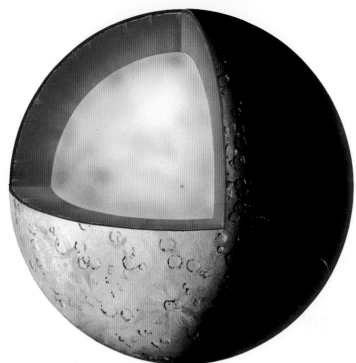

▶ Mercury's most unusual feature is its high density. Probably 70 percent of its mass is made up of iron, making it twice as rich in iron as any other planet. Most of this iron should exist in an enormous core with a diameter of around 2,250 miles (3,600 km), which is spinning, cooling and shrinking. The mantle is made of rocky **silicates**.

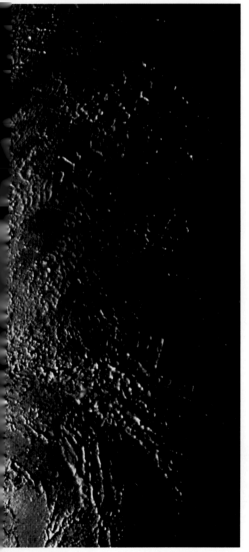

An enormous iron core

Mercury's **mass** is about 16 times smaller than that of the Earth. Its average density is about 5.4 times that of water. A weak **magnetic field** has been discovered (1 percent that of Earth's) that could be due to the rotation of a molten core of highly electrically-conductive iron.

Above the core lies a **mantle** of compressed, molten rocks, similar to the hot liquid rocks, or lavas, of the upper mantle that flow from volcanoes during eruptions on Earth. The solid surface, or crust, floats on the mantle. In our solar system, only Mercury, Venus, Earth and Mars have rocky surfaces. These are the terrestrial planets (from *terra*, the Latin word for Earth).

An airless world

Most planets have a layer of atmospheric gases above their surfaces, but Mercury, whose gravity is not strong enough to hold the gases around itself, is an almost airless world. The weight of an atmosphere is indicated by its pressure. Mercury's atmospheric pressure is one million millionth of Earth's! Only a few atoms, captured from the solar wind or escaping from the crust, are detected around the planet.

Because of the lack of atmosphere, which acts like a blanket, Mercury's surface does not remain warm at night, despite the high amount of solar energy heating it during the day. Variations of temperature between day and night, about 1,100°F (600°C), are greater than for any other planet in the solar system. During the long nights the temperature falls to about −330°F (−200°C), while long days produce a maximum of about 750°F (400°C), hot enough to melt tin or lead.

A surface like the Moon

The pictures of Mercury obtained by Mariner 10 show a surface very similar to the Moon's. There are countless impact craters, produced by numerous interplanetary bodies crashing into the surface, which is not protected by an atmospheric shield. In addition to the nine planets and their satellites, there are tens of thousands of smaller bodies in the solar system. Some, called asteroids, are made of rock and metal; others, called comets, consist mainly of dust and snow. When their orbits cross those of planets or satellites, they can hit the surface at great speed.

Mercury's surface is dotted with small bowl-shaped craters, less than 12 miles (20 km) wide. Larger craters have a central peak formed by the rock ejected from the surface. Huge craters, larger than 125 miles (200 km) wide, may have been flooded by fluid lavas from the mantle, to form relatively smooth, flat basins. The Caloris Basin is a flat, highly-cracked plain, about 800 miles (1,300 km) across, surrounded by ring-shaped mountains and **radial** valleys or ridges.

The mountains on Mercury are not as high as those on the Moon. It is thought most of the craters were formed soon after the formation of the solar system. Being so close to the Sun, Mercury then had a warm **plastic** crust, which led to the flattening of the cliffs around the impact craters. About 500 million years later, the small, cooling planet had shrunk, wrinkling parts of the surface to form cliffs, like the 300-mile (500-km) long Discovery Scarp, resulting in the harsh landscape seen today.

▶ Mountains surrounding the Caloris Basin rise above the cratered plains. The rims of circular fractures in the crust can be seen winding into the distance. The Sun, with its delicate corona and its halo of diffuse light, is visible against an otherwise black sky.

Venus

Surrounded by clouds floating in a dense, hot atmosphere, Venus is the second planet from the Sun. Every 19 months it comes closer to the Earth than any other planet and it is easily visible with the naked eye.

Difficult exploration

Venus has long been marveled at and observed during past centuries. However, the real exploration began in 1961, only four years after the first artificial satellite was launched. Until 1985, 18 Soviet unmanned spacecraft (16 named Venera and two Vega) have tried to explore Venus. The United States has sent six space probes (three Mariner, two Pioneer and the Magellan probe launched in May 1989) to the planet.

To reach Venus, with our present technology, requires a journey of about four to five months, and heat- and pressure-resistant vehicles are needed to land on the planet. Some spaceships have passed by Venus or have gone into orbit around it, others have sent probes or balloons deep into its heavy atmosphere. A few have landed on its surface, only surviving less than one hour, but the information they sent back to Earth revealed an impressive world.

A strange rotation

Because of the thickness of the clouds, the surface of Venus cannot be seen from the Earth or from any orbiter. Fortunately, radio waves pass through the clouds. The rotation can be measured by radar methods, similar to those used for Mercury.

Venus is the only planet in the solar system to spin backward, from east to west, very slowly. It takes 243 Earth days to complete one rotation around its axis. To observers on the surface (if they were able to see through the clouds), the Sun would rise in the west, and there would be daylight for 58 Earth days.

Facts about Venus	
Diameter	7,520 miles (12,100 km)
Mass	4/5 of the Earth's
Distance from the Sun	68 million miles (108 million km)
Period of rotation	243 days
Orbital period	225 days
Inclination of equator	2°
Surface gravity	9/10 of the Earth's
Temperature	900°F (500°C)
Atmosphere	97% carbon dioxide

▶ Space probe images of Venus, using ultraviolet light, show the upper regions of the thick clouds that completely cover the planet. Almost all of the incoming solar radiation is absorbed in the neighborhood of these cloud tops. The upper cloud layers on Venus rotate every four days, much faster than the rotation of the underlying planet.

The inset shows Venus as seen from Earth, with the naked eye. The planet appears white and featureless.

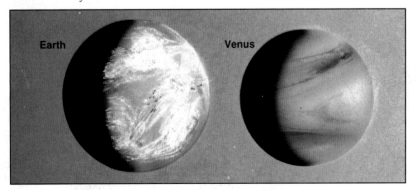

Earth   Venus

◀ The Earth and Venus are shown to scale. Venus's mass is four-fifths the Earth's and its diameter is 405 miles (650 km) less.

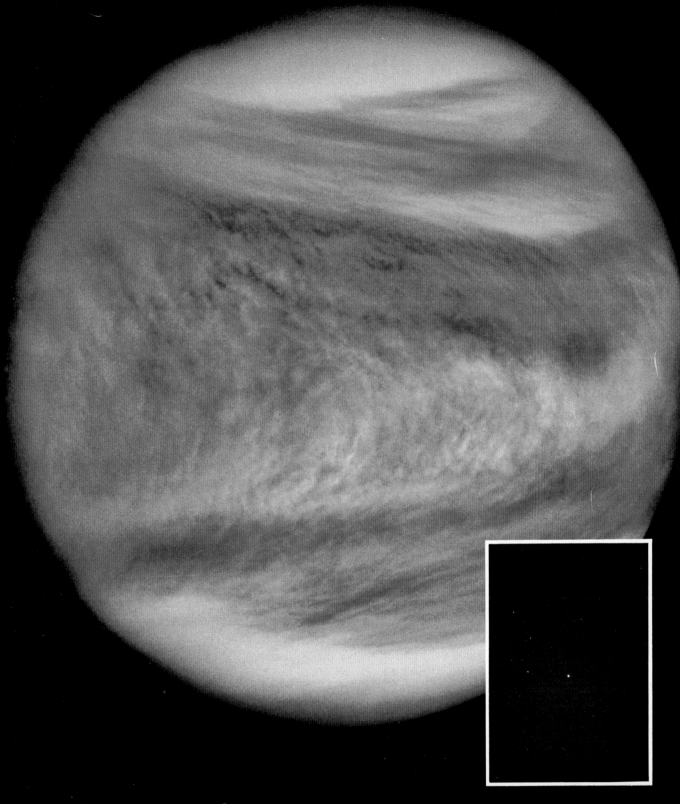

779   VENUS 0664   80 142   0419

Beneath yellow clouds

Neither a star...

Venus is often the brightest object in our sky after the Sun and the Moon. The shape of its sunlit face, observed through binoculars or through a telescope, changes as it revolves, displaying its several **phases**.

The angle between the Sun and Venus is never more than 47°, so the planet is only visible either at sunset or at sunrise. Though it is sometimes called the evening star or the morning star, in fact, Venus is not a star like the Sun, but a planet like Mercury or the Earth.

Nor Earth's twin sister...

Venus is 5 percent smaller and 19 percent less massive than Earth, so its density is almost the same as Earth's. Also Venus is closer to the Sun than is the Earth, but its cloud layers reflect more solar energy, so its surface receives about the same amount of solar radiation. One might think, therefore, that the two planets are alike, but they are very different.

Venus is named after the beautiful goddess of love, but the planet's surface is a dark, hot, suffocating inferno. The temperature of the surface is so great, 900°F (500°C), that it radiates like a microwave oven and would melt a metal like lead. Its atmosphere is mainly **carbon dioxide** and the atmospheric pressure on the surface (about 100 times the Earth's) would crush us.

A puzzling structure

The planet's interior is believed to be made up of a core of iron and **nickel**, a mantle of molten rocks and a solid crust. No magnetic field has been detected. With its high surface temperature, the venusian crust was thought to be thick and immovable. Some recently-discovered features, however, show that this crust might have broken into large pieces, or plates, which float and move on the mantle.

▶ The surface of Venus is stiflingly hot and lies under a heavy atmosphere containing many cloud layers encircling the planet. This is a view above the surface of the eerily-lit, once volcanic region, near the poles. A rare, temporary clearing in the lower clouds gives a brief glimpse of the Sun.

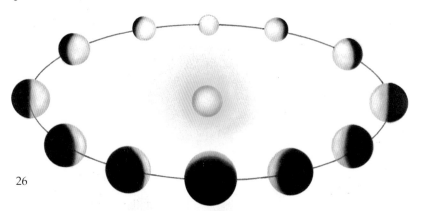

◀ From Earth we see a continually changing view of Venus. The planet goes through a series of phases, just like our Moon. We see only the portion of the planet that is lit by sunlight. When it is close to Earth, Venus appears much larger than when it is on the other side of its orbit.

mantle

core

▶ Below the surface, Venus's composition is similar to Earth's. Its iron-nickel core, which is probably molten, is surrounded by a thick rock mantle on which floats a crust.

crust

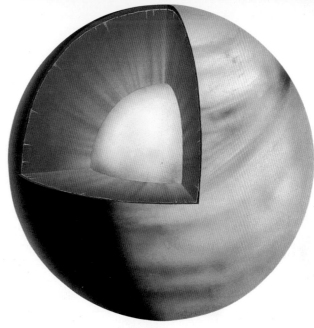

27

The rocky desert surface

▼ Looking from the western wall of a wide, winding valley, Devana Chasma, the great **shield volcano**, Theia Mons (now extinct), is seen pouring enormous billows of ash into the sky. Lightning bolts crackle in the volcanic dust plume, and the fiery landscape is dotted with lakes of molten lava.

An infernal atmosphere

If a probe were to float down through Venus's dense, choking atmosphere it would first cross three thick layers of yellow-white clouds and haze, between 40 and 30 miles (70 and 50 km) above the surface. The clouds are made of tiny drops of poisonous, corrosive, liquid sulfuric acid, and are known to streak by at almost 250 miles an hour (400 km an hour), circling the planet in four days.

Below the cloud layers, the probe would travel through a dark red transparent atmosphere where it would eventually observe electric discharges and lightning. The venusian atmosphere consists of 97 percent carbon dioxide, with traces of **nitrogen**, **water vapor**, and **argon**. Carbon dioxide gas is transparent to visible light, but opaque to the **infrared** radiation from the Sun. Incoming solar radiation is absorbed by the carbon dioxide, which causes the intense heat of the planet's surface. Venus's lower atmosphere acts like a greenhouse.

▼ The Soviet spacecraft Venera 10 can be seen coming in to land on a flat expanse of dark soil, partially covered with wide, irregular, flat slabs of lighter, crusty rock. The spacecraft is built like a diving bell so that it can withstand the atmospheric pressure. It was initially slowed down by parachutes but the sombrero-like rim provided the braking for the final descent. Once on the surface, the spacecraft could operate for approximately one hour before succumbing to the effects of the heat, pressure and the acid that condensed on it as it passed through the clouds.

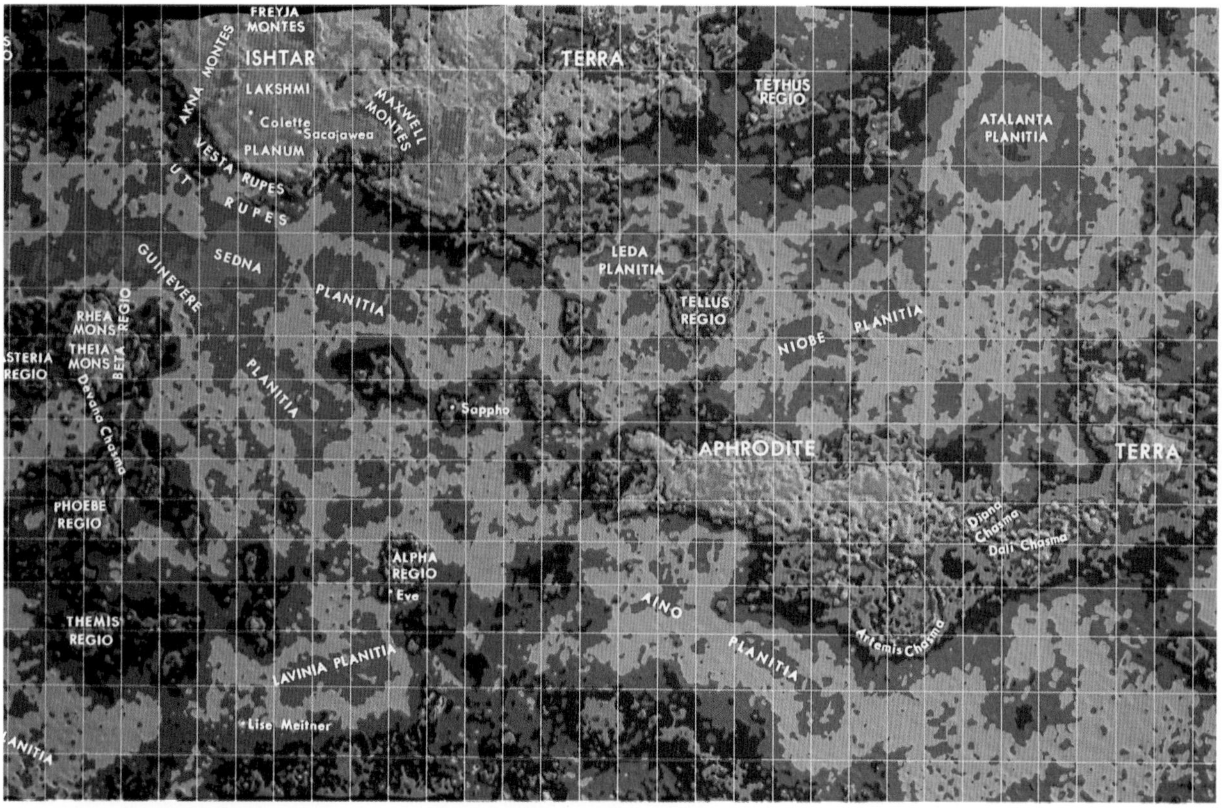
FREYJA MONTES
ISHTAR
TERRA
LAKSHMI
Colette
Sacajawea
PLANUM
AKNA MONTES
MAXWELL MONTES
VESTA RUPES
UT RUPES
TETHUS REGIO
ATALANTA PLANITIA
SEDNA
PLANITIA
GUINEVERE
PLANITIA
LEDA PLANITIA
TELLUS REGIO
NIOBE
PLANITIA
RHEA MONS
THEIA MONS
BETA REGIO
STERIA REGIO
Devana Chasma
Sappho
APHRODITE
TERRA
PHOEBE REGIO
ALPHA REGIO
Eve
Diana Chasma
Dali Chasma
AINO
PLANITIA
Artemis Chasma
THEMIS REGIO
LAVINIA PLANITIA
Lise Meitner
ANITIA

▲ The radar signal from the Pioneer Orbiter penetrated the clouds above Venus and the information obtained has been used to draw this color contour map. Each color represents a 0.6-mile (1-km) contour. Deep blue is the lowest region, followed by green, yellow, orange and red. The Ishtar Terra plain is about the size of Australia, and Aphrodite Terra, the size of Africa.

Varied landscape

Radar maps of Venus have been obtained from the Pioneer Venus 1, Venera 15 and Venera 16 orbiters, by bouncing radio waves off the surface, revealing vast areas of land, like Earth's continents. About 70 percent of the surface is a hot desert of high, rolling plains. Lying below the plains are lowlands (about 20 percent of the surface) that can be compared to the sea bottom on Earth. Highlands rise above the plains, making up 10 percent of the surface. Aphrodite, a region of land as wide as Africa, is remarkable for its deep and long **rift valleys**. Ishtar, wider than Australia, is unique for the huge Maxwell mountain, higher than Mount Everest. Beta Regio is comprised mostly of the mountain ranges, Theia and Rhea, which seem to be of volcanic origin.

Panoramic photographs of the rolling plains' rocky surface, taken by the Venera 9, 10, 13 and 14 landers, show a dark gray surface of boulders and sand. Chemical analysis reveals most of the rocks to be volcanic **basalts**, probably worn down by wind-blown material and acid in the atmosphere.

Although our knowledge of the planet has increased with space exploration, Venus remains mysterious. Is there volcanic activity today? Were its crater-like features caused by asteroids and comets hitting the surface? Perhaps future technology will help us understand this forbidding world.

Earth

Earth is the third planet from the Sun, orbiting in the **ecliptic plane** at 18 miles a second (30 km a second). It makes one revolution in 365.25 days, which explains why our year, usually 365 days long, has 366 days every 4 years.

The Earth rotates once around its axis in about 24 hours, circling the Sun at the same time. The length of night and day changes with the seasons. As our planet orbits the Sun, the northern end of its polar axis (the North Pole) always points to the same spot in the sky, near the North Star. During summer in the northern hemisphere, the North Pole is closest to the Sun. North America, Europe, northern Africa and Asia receive more direct sunlight than South America, southern Africa or Australia.

Journey to the center of the Earth

When the Earth was formed 4,600 million years ago, the heavy metals sank to its center, and lighter material moved to the outside. The interior structure of the Earth is deduced from studying earthquakes. Both the density and the temperature increase with depth. The Earth's interior is still hot, because of the **radioactivity** of some of its rocks. The solid rocky surface, or crust, is usually a few miles (km) thick below our feet, but is thinner under the oceans. Below the crust lies a fluid mantle. Because of the high temperature and pressure, the rocks in the mantle are plastic and five times as dense as water. The core's temperature is about 5,400°F (3,000°C) with a density eleven times that of water. At its center the core could be solid iron, surrounded by liquid iron with some nickel and **sulfur**.

The **conductive**, rotating iron and nickel inside the planet acts like a huge magnet with its **poles** very near the geographic poles. In fact, a compass needle does not turn to the north geographic pole, but to the magnetic pole.

Facts about the Earth

Diameter	7,926 miles (12,756km)
Mass	$5,975 \times 10^{21}$ tons (tonnes)
Distance from the Sun	94 million miles (150 million km)
Period or rotation	23 h 56 mins
Orbital period	365.25 days
Inclination of equator	23.44°
Temperature	72°F (22°C) (average)
Atmosphere	78% nitrogen, 21% oxygen

▶ Looking down on our own planet, Earth, we see afternoon in the eastern Mediterranean and midnight on the west coast of America. The beautiful, hazy arc of light circling the North Pole is the aurora borealis. These "northern lights" dancing in the sky are caused by energetic particles colliding with atoms and molecules in our upper atmosphere as they are pushed from the radiation belts surrounding our planet. On the dark side of the Earth the red glow of burning gas from oilfields contrasts with the bright lights of the cities.

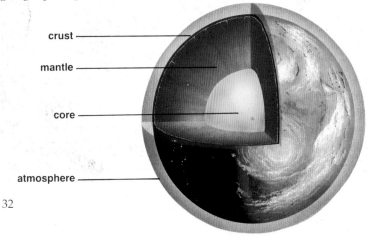

crust —
mantle —
core —
atmosphere —

◀ Beneath the Earth's crust is a mantle of rock and a core of solid iron surrounded by a layer of liquid iron.

A restless world

Since the Earth formed, mountains have been worn down by rains, sand dunes moved by winds, canyons carved by rivers, valleys filled with soil, new mountains or islands built by volcanic lavas. Even the shapes and location of the continents have changed.

If you compare on a map the eastern shore of South America and the western shore of Africa, the two coastlines almost fit together. Seventy million years ago, the ten enormous pieces, or plates, of the Earth's crust were much closer together. They are now floating about on the hot liquid mantle, and volcanoes and earthquakes occur along their boundaries.

In places, plates bump together and one slides over the other, rocks fold up and new mountains appear. The Himalayas were formed when the Indian plate collided with the Asian plate. In other regions, plates are pushed apart, along rifts produced by molten rocks flowing from the mantle below the oceans. Such volcanic activity has caused a long submarine ridge in the middle of the Atlantic Ocean, marking the boundary between the three plates carrying Europe, Africa and America.

A unique atmosphere

The surface of our planet is unique in the solar system because two-thirds is covered with wide oceans of liquid water. On Venus, water would boil away; on Mars, it would freeze. Earth's atmosphere is also unique because of the quantity of **oxygen**, generated billions of years ago by **algae** growing in the oceans. When the solar system formed, our atmosphere was mainly hydrogen and helium, but these light gases escaped rapidly.

A new atmosphere formed consisting of carbon dioxide, water vapor and nitrogen. On planet Earth the water vapor condensed rapidly, and it rained heavily for centuries all over the world, forming the oceans, into which the carbon dioxide dissolved.

The lower atmosphere

The air we breathe is a mixture of mainly nitrogen and oxygen, and small amounts of

▼ All landmasses were probably assembled in one supercontinent, Pangea, 280 million years ago, as shown below.

▼ Around 160 million years ago, Pangea split into five continents, North America, Europe, Siberia, China and Gondwanaland.

argon, carbon dioxide, helium and water vapor, which condenses to form rain in low clouds and snow in high clouds. Water is constantly exchanged between the atmosphere and oceans. Clouds, rain, thunderstorms and snow only occur up to about 7 miles (12 km) above the surface, a region called the **troposphere**. Here the temperature decreases with increasing height, which is why high mountains are often covered with snow.

The atmospheric shield

Above the troposphere is the **stratosphere**, where the temperature increases slightly. The stratosphere is very important for our survival. A thin layer of ozone gas 21 miles (35 km) above the Earth's surface shields the ground from harmful ultraviolet radiation. The ozone is formed when ultraviolet sunlight breaks atmospheric oxygen into atoms which collide. All the harmful radiation is absorbed before reaching the troposphere.

Atmospheric pressure decreases with increasing height. At about 4 miles (6 km), the air is too thin for humans to breathe easily. At higher altitudes we need pressurized air to survive, so these regions have been extensively explored by airplanes, balloons, rockets and satellites.

Our atmosphere extends up to 300 miles (500 km) high, but a few atmospheric particles are found even higher. When the electrically-charged atoms of the solar wind reach the upper atmosphere, they are deflected by the Earth's magnetic field, the **magnetosphere**, which extends out to 60,000 miles (100,000 km) on the day side of the planet, and even farther on the night side.

Life on planet Earth

The first microscopic creatures appeared thousands of millions of years ago in the oceans. Blue-green algae used sunlight to convert the dissolved carbon dioxide into sugar and energy, by **photosynthesis**, giving out oxygen as a waste product.

About 500 million years ago, enough oxygen had accumulated in the atmosphere to allow life to spread from the oceans onto the land. Millions of years passed during which the first fish, insects, amphibians, reptiles and dinosaurs appeared. Birds and mammals evolved 300 million years ago, and the earliest known humans 2 million years ago.

To live, we need oxygen and liquid water, so it is most likely that the Earth is the only planet in the solar system where creatures like ourselves, elaborate life-forms, exist today.

▼ The continents moved farther apart, but South America is still joined to the Antarctic and the Isthmus of Panama has not yet formed.

▼ In this picture, we can see the new Atlantic Ocean getting bigger, while the Pacific Ocean is getting smaller.

The growth of life

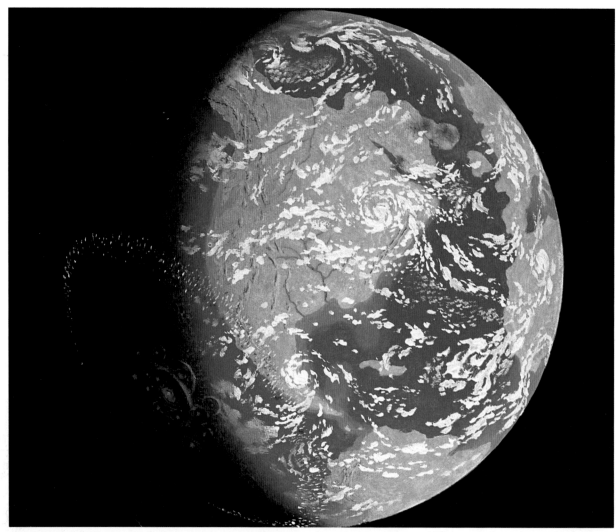

◀ This painting shows the scene around 38 million years ago when a huge comet or asteroid has just struck the Earth. Material that has been ejected from the crater is falling back to the surface. Such an event may be responsible for the death of the dinosaurs. It is possible that a huge forest fire followed the impact, throwing dust up into the atmosphere, causing a prolonged global winter and a massive loss of vegetation.

▼ Charles Darwin suggested that men, monkeys and apes have a common ancestry. About 38 million years ago, the hominoids, from which we are descended, branched off from the other primates. In this picture we see our possible ancestors as they may have been 10 million years ago. This branch of the hominoids, the dryopithecines, had small monkey-like brains and could walk erect. The first true man, Homo sapiens, inhabited Earth around 400,000 years ago.

The growth of technology

▲ This is how North and South America look today. The state of our development is illustrated by the city in the lower section. We might take electric lighting, telephone communication and intercontinental jet planes for granted, but this modern life-style has only existed for a minute fraction of the total lifetime of our planet.

▼ Moving several years into the future, the large quantity of light coming from the night side of our planet underlines the fact that the population of Earth has increased alarmingly.
One of our major preoccupations is the constant search for new sources of energy.
The space workers are constructing a huge solar panel in near-Earth orbit, which will convert sunlight into electricity to be radiated down to Earth by microwave links.

Spaceship Earth

The Earth's atmosphere provides the air we breathe, shields us from harmful radiation, and keeps the surface warm. It also protects us from all but the largest incoming asteroids.

You may have seen flashes of light shooting across the night sky. These are meteors (fragments of asteroids or comets) that are slowed down by the atmosphere and vaporized. Most of these rocks burn up before reaching the surface, which is why there are few impact craters on Earth, but occasionally a large fragment may hit the land or splash into the ocean.

Some scientists believe that such impacts, more than 4,000 million years ago, contributed to the amount of water on the Earth's surface, as the mass of a comet is mostly water ice. Others argue that they played a role in the disappearance of the dinosaurs, 60 million years ago. As comets or asteroids hit the surface, enormous amounts of dust and debris released into the atmosphere might have drastically altered the weather, blocking out the Sun.

Much more recently, on June 30, 1908, a ball of fire crossed the sky above Siberia and a frightening explosion took place. Sunshine was masked by dust, while trees were destroyed and burned over vast areas. The cause was probably a small comet or asteroid that had disintegrated in the lower atmosphere. Eyewitnesses to the "Tunguska Event" told of a long, flaming, red object, wreathed by puffs of smoke and blue streamers producing great heat, noise and strong winds.

Though our atmosphere protects us from many of these collisions, it is possible that one day *we* may destroy our unique atmospheric shield. The thin ozone layer is being pierced by chemicals, resulting in increased harmful solar radiation. An increase in carbon dioxide from pollution may absorb and trap infrared radiation, leading to a catastrophic greenhouse effect (as on Venus), a waterless Earth and the disappearance of life. It is important that we realize the effects that mankind has had on our beautiful blue planet and that we do what we can to preserve life on our fragile spaceship.

▶ The enormous explosion that took place at Tunguska was thought to have been caused by a comet hitting the Earth. The comet probably had a nucleus of dust and snow about 130 feet (40 m) wide. The main explosion took place at the point where the nucleus first slowed down, 5 miles (8 km) above the Earth's surface. The explosive force was equivalent to 12.5 megatons of TNT. The ancient trees of the mighty Yenissi Taiga were torn up by their roots. No craters were formed, because the explosion took place high in the atmosphere. The devastation extended over an area with a radius of 25 miles (40 km). The central region was ravaged by a fire with a radius of 11 miles (18 km).

▶ This is how our planet might look when its water, plants, clouds and atmosphere have been lost. Fortunately this is not likely to happen for millions of years. An extraterrestrial astronomer would deduce from this picture that the Earth's crust was in constant motion and highlands and lowlands were constantly shifting. Collisions between land plates produce mountain ranges like the American Rockies. Trenches are also produced; new crust can be seen emerging along the Mid-Atlantic Ridge.

Glossary

algae: simple plants without proper leaves or stems which live in damp places, stagnant water or the sea.

angular diameter: the ratio of the diameter of a planet, star or moon to its distance from the observer. The Moon appears the same size as the Sun in our sky because, although considerably smaller, it is much nearer to Earth.

argon: a colorless, odorless gas.

auroras: lights which appear in our sky around the north and south magnetic poles, when solar flare particles invade the magnetosphere.

basalt: a dark gray or black fine-grained rock formed when magma solidifies.

carbon dioxide: a gas made up of one atom of carbon joined to two atoms of oxygen. All animals breathe out carbon dioxide, and plants use carbon dioxide to make food.

chromosphere: a layer of gas that makes up part of the Sun's atmosphere. It has a pinkish color.

conductive: material that is able to direct or transmit forms of energy. A copper wire conducts electricity; metals conduct heat well.

convection: the movement of heat in a liquid or gas. The hot liquid or gas rises to the top; the cold sinks to the bottom. The process is continuous and a convection current is set up.

core: the center of something.

corona: a faint halo of the glowing gases that surround the Sun.

coronagraph: a telescope that masks out the Sun's disc.

density: the mass of a substance divided by its volume (i.e. iron is twice as dense as rock and rock is 3.3 times as dense as water, so water has a lower density than rock).

disc: as planets, the Moon and the Sun are much closer to us than stars, they appear as small discs when you look at them. Stars appear as points.

eclipse: happens when one object blocks off the light from another. In a solar eclipse, the Moon comes between the Sun and the Earth. In a lunar eclipse, the Moon passes into the Earth's shadow.

ecliptic plane: the annual apparent path of the Sun across the sky; the plane of the orbit of the Earth around the Sun.

elliptical: oval-shaped.

flare: a sudden, bright outburst of energy.

frequency: the number of vibrations (usually per second) in a wave motion. The greater the frequency in sound waves, the higher the pitch of sound. There is a wide range of radio waves, all with different frequencies. The greater the frequency in light waves, the bluer the color.

gravity: the force that pulls objects towards each other. The Sun's gravity keeps the Earth in orbit around it. The Earth's gravity keeps us on the Earth. The gravitational field of a body is the space surrounding that body within which its gravity affects other bodies.

infrared: waves which have shorter frequencies than the red light waves we see, but longer than radio waves. We feel them as heat.

ionize: to convert into ions (groups of atoms that have a positive or negative charge).

magnetic field: a region where a magnetic force is acting.

magnetosphere: the region of the Earth's environment in which we are protected from the ionized particles in the solar wind.

mantle: the layer of molten rock between the outer shell (crust) of a planet and its core.

mass: the quantity of material in an object.

nickel: a hard silvery-white metal easily beaten into shapes.

nitrogen: a colorless, odorless, tasteless gas that does not burn.

nuclear fusion: the center of an atom is its nucleus. The nuclei of many atoms can join together in a process called fusion. This makes atoms much heavier and releases a great amount of energy. Fusion makes the Sun burn.

orbital plane: the flat surface that contains the orbital path of the planet as it moves around the Sun.

oxygen: the gas which is in air and water. All animal and plant life uses oxygen in order to live.

penumbra: the lighter shadow surrounding the umbra caused by the light source being only partially obscured.

period of revolution: the time taken for a planet or other object to travel once around another object.

period of rotation: the time taken for a planet or other object to spin once around its axis.

phase: the change in the apparent shape of a moon or planet made by the reflection of the Sun's light.

photosphere: the surface of the Sun that we can see. It is made of hot gases and gives off almost all of the light we get from the Sun.

photosynthesis: in green plants, the making (synthesis) of soluble plant foods (mainly sugars) from carbon dioxide and water, using energy from sunlight.

plastic: a material or substance that changes shape under a force but keeps shape when the force is removed.

polar axis: an imaginary straight line drawn between the most northern and southern points of a spinning object. The object revolves around this line.

poles: the most northern, or southern, points on a planet, star or moon.

prism: a solid shape with equal, parallel triangular ends and three sides that are parallelograms. A piece of glass shaped like a prism will break up light passing through it into the colors of the rainbow.

prominence: a bright spot of gas reaching from the Sun's surface, or photosphere, out into space.

radar: a system of bouncing radio waves off an object and timing their return to calculate how far away the object is. Radar is short for **ra**dio **d**etecting **an**d **r**anging.

radial: rays coming from a common center.

radioactivity: heavy elements giving off harmful radiation in the form of waves or particles as the atomic nuclei break up.

red giant: a red star many times greater in size than our Sun in which the supply of fuel has

become low. The star becomes larger and cooler, but its core becomes hotter.

rift valleys: cracks, or faults, in the crust along which the land has slipped down.

shield volcano: a volcano with a shape resembling the shields of ancient Viking warriors.

silicates: salts obtained from silica, a hard crystalline mineral substance found in flint, quartz and sand.

spectroscope: an instrument that measures the amount of light an object reflects by breaking up the light into the colors of the visible spectrum.

spectroscopy: the application of the results obtained from a spectroscope in determining the composition of a light-reflecting object.

spectrum: the rainbow-colored bands of light seen when white light is split up by water droplets in the atmosphere, or by a prism. The bands are arranged in order of frequency; red is the shortest, violet is the longest, visible wave.

stratosphere: the layer of the Earth's atmosphere, above the troposphere, extending from 7 to 31 miles (12 to 50 km) above the surface.

streamers: long narrow ribbons of energy or light-reflecting particles.

sulfur: a hard, brittle, yellow substance that burns with a blue flame and forms an unpleasant-smelling gas.

sunspot: a dark patch which marks cooler gases on the surface of the Sun.

troposphere: the layer of the Earth's atmosphere extending from the surface up to 5 miles (8 km) at the poles and 11 miles (18 km) above the equatorial regions. The troposphere contains all the weather systems and clouds.

ultraviolet: radiation with a greater frequency than the violet light we see. Ultraviolet radiation occurs naturally in sunlight and is invisible, but can be harmful to plant and animal life.

umbra: the darkest part of the shadow caused by a solar eclipse. An observer in the umbra can see no part of the source of light.

water vapor: water in the form of a gas. Water vapor is always present in the air.

Index

oxygen, 34, 35
ozone, 35, 40

P
partial eclipse, 11, 14
period of revolution, 6, 18, 32
period of rotation, 16, 18,
     24, 32
phase 26
photosphere, 8, 16
photosynthesis, 35
Pioneer spacecraft, 24, 31
plates, 26, 34
Pluto, 18
polar axis, 16
prism, 7
prominence, 10, 17

R
radar, 18, 24, 31
red giant star, 8
Rhea mountains, 31
rift valleys, 31, 34
rolling plains, 31

S
satellite, 6, 17, 22, 24
Saturn, 6
season, 32
shooting star, 40
solar cycle, 16, 17
solar eclipse, 10, 11, 12, 14
solar system, 6, 22, 34
solar wind, 17, 21, 35
spectroscope, 7
spectroscopy, 7
spectrum, 7

stratosphere, 35
sulfur, 32
sulfuric acid, 30
Sun
   atmosphere, 10
   composition, 7, 8, 10, 16, 17
   core, 8
   rotation, period of, 16
sunspot, 16, 17

T
terrestrial planet, 21
Theia mountains, 31
total eclipse, 11, 14
troposphere, 35

U
ultraviolet radiation, 14, 24, 35

V
Vega spacecraft, 24
Venera spacecraft, 24, 30, 31
Venus
   atmosphere, 26, 30
   core, 26, 27
   crust, 26, 27, 30
   mantle, 26
   revolution, period of, 24
   rotation, period of, 24
volcano, 29, 31, 34

W
water vapor, 30, 34, 35
wave, 18, 24

X
X-ray, 14

Acknowledgments

ILLUSTRATIONS
6, 7, 9, 10, 12, 13, 14, 15, 16,
17, 19, 23, 27, 28, 29, 30,
34, 35, 36, 37, 38, 39, 41 top
and bottom: Don Davis.
11, 26: Sebastian Quigley/
Linden Artists.

PHOTOGRAPHIC CREDITS
8: BLA. 20: NASA/Science
Photo Library.
25: NASA. 25 inset: John Sanford/
31: NASA/ Science Photo Library.
Science Photo Library.